C0-ANC-108

Program Authors

Peter Afflerbach

Camille Blachowicz

Candy Dawson Boyd

Elena Izquierdo

Connie Juel

Edward Kame'enui

Donald Leu

Jeanne R. Paratore

P. David Pearson

Sam Sebesta

Deborah Simmons

Alfred Tatum

Sharon Vaughn

Susan Watts Taffe

Karen Kring Wixson

PEARSON

Glenview, Illinois • Boston, Massachusetts • Chandler, Arizona •
Upper Saddle River, New Jersey

We dedicate Reading Street to
Peter Jovanovich.

His wisdom, courage,
and passion for education
are an inspiration to us all.

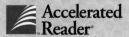

About the Cover Artist
Rob Hefferan likes to reminisce about the simple life he had as a child growing up in Cheshire, when his biggest worry was whether to have fish fingers or Alphabetti Spaghetti for tea. The faces, colors, and shapes from that time are a present-day inspiration for his artwork.

Copyright © 2011 by Pearson Education, Inc., or its affiliates. All Rights Reserved. Printed in the United States of America. This publication is protected by copyright, and permission should be obtained from the publisher prior to any prohibited reproduction, storage in a retrieval system, or transmission in any form or by any means, electronic, mechanical, photocopying, recording, or likewise. For information regarding permissions, write to Pearson Curriculum Group Rights & Permissions, One Lake Street, Upper Saddle River, New Jersey 07458.

Pearson, Scott Foresman, and Pearson Scott Foresman are trademarks, in the U.S. and/or other countries, of Pearson Education, Inc., or its affiliates.

ISBN-13: 978-0-328-47851-4
ISBN-10:   0-328-47851-2
2 3 4 5 6 7 8 9 10 V042 14 13 12 11 10
CC1

Dear Texas Reader,

Hold on to your thinking caps! Our next trip on Reading Street is all about adventure! We will see the world with a rooster, travel to the coldest place on Earth, and fly over New York City. Are you ready?

AlphaBuddy says, "Remember those letters and words you've learned. You'll need them."

Keep up the good work!

Sincerely,
The Authors

Let's Go Exploring

 Where will our adventures take us?

Big Book

4

Week 2

Trade Book

Animal Fantasy • Social Studies
My Lucky Day by Keiko Kasza

Unit 4 Contents

Week 3

Week 4

Week 5

Week 6

Don Leu
The Internet Guy

Right before our eyes, the nature of reading and learning is changing. The Internet and other technologies create new opportunities, new solutions, and new literacies. New reading comprehension skills are required online. They are increasingly important to our students and our society.

Those of us on the Reading Street team are here to help you on this new, and very exciting, journey.

See It!

- Big Question Video

- Concept Talk Video

- Envision It! Animations

- eReaders

Hear It!

- *Sing with Me Animations*

- eSelections

- Grammar Jammer

Adam and Kim play at the beach.

Concept Talk Video

File   Edit   View   Favorites   Tools   Help

http://www.TexasReadingStreet.com

Do It!

- Story Sort

- eReaders

- Letter Tile Drag and Drop   o s c m s

Let's Go Exploring

TEXAS
Reading Street **Online**

www.TexasReadingStreet.com
• Big Question Video
• Envision It! Animations
• Story Sort

THE BIG
?

Where will our adventures take us?

TEKS

K.2.E.1 Recognize spoken alliteration or groups of words that begin with the same spoken onset or initial sound. **K.2.F.1** Blend spoken onsets and rimes to form simple words. **K.2.H.1** Isolate the initial sound in spoken one-syllable words.

Phonemic Awareness

Let's Listen for

Read Together

Initial Sounds

● Point to a hand. Say the word. Say the beginning sound.

■ Find three things that begin with /h/, like *hand*.

▲ Point to these pictures and say the words: *hanger, hippo, hair.* Do they begin the same? What about *shoe, leg, house?*

★ Point to the hat. Say /h/ *-at.* Blend the word. Change /h/ to /b/. Blend the new word.

READING STREET ONLINE
BIG QUESTION VIDEO
www.TexasReadingStreet.com

Envision It!

Sequence

READING STREET ONLINE
ENVISION IT! ANIMATIONS
www.TexasReadingStreet.com

14

TEKS

K.3.A.1 Identify the common sounds that letters represent. **K.3.B.1** Use letter-sound relationships to decode regular words in text and independent of content. **K.3.D.1** Identify and read at least 25 high-frequency words from a commonly used list.

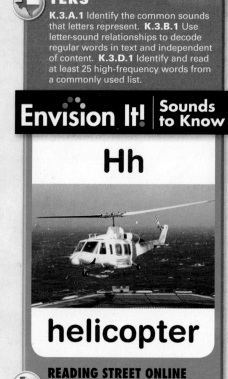

Envision It! | Sounds to Know

Hh

helicopter

READING STREET ONLINE ALPHABET CARDS
www.TexasReadingStreet.com

Phonics

Initial *Hh*

Words I Can Blend

h i d

Words I Can Read

are

that

do

Sentences I Can Read

1. They are hot.
2. That hat is for him.
3. Do you like the hat?

TEKS
K.3.A.1 Identify the common sounds that letters represent. **K.3.B.1** Use knowledge of letter-sound relationships to decode regular words in text. **K.3.D** Identify and read at least 25 high-frequency words from a commonly used list.

Phonics

I Can Read!

Decodable Reader

- Consonant *Hh*
  Hob
  hit
  hot
  had
  hat

- High-Frequency Words
  that
  is
  do
  see
  a
  they
  are

▲ Read the story.

READING STREET ONLINE
DECODABLE eREADERS
www.TexasReadingStreet.com

Hob Can Hit

Written by Roy Kass
Illustrated by Ryan Bines

Decodable Reader 19

That man is Dan Hob.
Hob can hit.
Hob can do it!

That fan is Pam.
Can Pam see Hob?
Pam can.

That fan is Sam.
Can Sam see Hob?
Sam can.

Did Hob hit it?
Hob did not.

Did Hob hit it?
Hob did not.

Hob is hot.
Hob had a hat.

Pop! Hob hit it!
Hob did it!
They are not sad.

TEKS

K.6.A.3 Identify elements of a story including key events. **K.8.A.1** Retell a main event from a story read aloud. **RC-K.E.1** Retell important events in stories.

Envision It! | Retell

Big Book

Rooster's Off to See the World

1

2

3

4

5

6

Think, Talk, and Write

1. Would you choose to see the world with Rooster? Why or why not? **Text to Self**

2. What does Rooster do first in the story? What does he do last?

Sequence

3. Look back and write.

TEKS

K.5.A Identify and use words that name sequences. **K.21.A.1** Listen attentively by facing speakers. **K.21.B.1** Follow oral directions that involve a short related sequence of actions.

Vocabulary

- Talk about the pictures.

- ■ What did you do before school?

- ▲ What will you do after school?

- ★ Form a line. Who is at the beginning of the line? Who is at the end?

Listening and Speaking

- Point to AlphaBuddy's nose.

- ■ Point to AlphaBuddy's mouth.

- ▲ Point to AlphaBuddy's ear.

- ★ Point to AlphaBuddy's foot.

Vocabulary

Sequence Words

before

after

beginning

end

Give Directions

Be a good speaker!

TEKS

K.4.B.2 Respond to questions about texts read aloud. K.6.D Recognize recurring phrases and characters in traditional lullabies from various cultures. RC-K.A.2 Discuss the purposes for listening to various texts.

The Evening Is Coming

Let's Practice It!

Lullaby

● Listen to the lullaby.

■ Which lines repeat?

▲ What animals are mentioned in this lullaby? What are they doing?

★ What is the purpose of a lullaby? How does a lullaby do that?

30

TEKS

K.2.E.1 Recognize spoken alliteration or groups of words that begin with the same spoken onset or initial sound. **K.2.F1** Blend spoken onsets and rimes to form simple words. **K.2.H.1** Isolate the initial sound in spoken one-syllable words.

Phonemic Awareness

Let's Listen for

Initial Sounds

Read Together

● Point to the loaf of bread. Say *loaf*. Say the beginning sound.

■ Point to the bell. Say *bell*. Say the ending sound.

▲ Find three things that begin with /l/. Find three things that end with /l/.

★ Point to these things and say the words: *leg, lid, lap*. Do they begin the same? Do these words end the same: *girl, fill, doll*?

♥ Blend /f/ -ill. What is the word? Yes, *fill*. Change /f/ to /w/. Blend the new word.

READING STREET ONLINE
BIG QUESTION VIDEO
www.TexasReadingStreet.com

33

Comprehension

Envision It!

Cause and Effect

**READING STREET ONLINE
ENVISION IT! ANIMATIONS**
www.TexasReadingStreet.com

34

TEKS

K.3.B Use knowledge of letter-sound relationships to decode regular words in text and independent of content.
K.3.C.2 Recognize that new words are created when letters are added.

Envision It! | **Sounds to Know**

Ll

lemon

READING STREET ONLINE ALPHABET CARDS
www.TexasReadingStreet.com

Phonics

Initial and Final *Ll*

Words I Can Blend

l a d

l i d

l o t

i l l

f i l l

Words I Can Read

are

that

do

Sentences I Can Read

1. That man is my dad.

2. We are on the hill.

3. Do you hop a lot?

TEKS

K.3.A.1 Identify the common sounds that letters represent. **K.3.B.1** Use knowledge of letter-sound relationships to decode regular words in text. **K.3.D** Identify and read at least 25 high-frequency words from a commonly used list.

Phonics

I Can Read!

Decodable Reader

- Consonant *Ll*
  lap
  Lil
  lit
  doll
  lid

- High-Frequency Words

a	do
you	see
the	they
that	are

▲ Read the story.

READING STREET ONLINE
DECODABLE eREADERS
www.TexasReadingStreet.com

Can It Fit?

Written by Myleen Rush
Illustrated by Gloria Leek

Decodable Reader 20

Tab sat on a lap.
Kit did not.

Lil lit it.

Do you see Tab?

Lil had a doll.
Kit can bat it.

Kit sat in the lid.
Can Tab fit?

They fit in that lid.

Can Tab fit on Lil?
Can Kit fit on Lil?

They are on Lil.

TEKS

K.8.A.1 Retell a main event from a story read aloud. **K.8.B.2** Describe reasons [for characters'] actions. **RC-K.E.1** Retell important events in stories. **RC-K.F.1** Make connections to own experiences.

Envision It! | Retell

Trade Book

Think, Talk, and Write

1. Tell about a lucky adventure you have had.

Text to Self

2. What does the fox do to the piglet? Why does he do this?

Cause and Effect

3. Look back and write.

TEKS

K.5.C Identify and sort pictures of objects into conceptual categories. **K.21.A.1** Listen attentively by facing speakers. **K.23.A.2** Follow agreed-upon rules for discussion, including speaking one at a time.

Let's Learn It!

Vocabulary

- ● Talk about the pictures.
- ■ Find things that are fuzzy.
- ▲ Find things that are bumpy.
- ★ Find things that are furry.
- ♥ Find things that are sharp.

Listening and Speaking

- ● How are breakfast and dinner alike?
- ■ How are breakfast and dinner different?
- ▲ How are a pig and a fox alike?
- ★ How are a pig and a fox different?

Vocabulary

Words for Textures

fuzzy

bumpy

sharp

furry

48

Compare and Contrast

TEKS

K.6.B Discuss the big idea (theme) of a well-known fable and connect it to personal experience. **K.8.B.2** Describe reasons for characters' actions. **RC-K.F** Make connections to own experiences and discuss textual evidence.

The Crow and the Pitcher

Let's Practice It!

Fable

- ● Listen to the fable.
- ■ Why can't the crow get the water in the pitcher?
- ▲ Why does the crow drop pebbles into the pitcher?
- ★ What lesson does the fable teach?
- ♥ What new expression does this fable teach you?
- ● When have you done something a little at a time? Tell about it.

1

2

51

TEKS

K.2.E.1 Recognize spoken alliteration or groups of words that begin with the same spoken onset or initial sound. **K.2.F.1** Blend spoken onsets and rimes to form simple words.

Phonemic Awareness

Let's Listen for

Initial Sounds

Read Together

- Point to the sled. Say *sled*. Say the blended sound at the beginning: /s/ /l/, /sl/.

- Point to the plow. Say *plow*. Say the blended sound at the beginning: /p/ /l/, /pl/.

- Find things that begin with /sl/, /pl/, /bl/, /gl/, /fl/.

- Say these words: *spin, spell, speak*. Do they begin the same? What about *crack, crash, skate*?

- Blend /sl/ -ip. What's the word? Yes, *slip*. Change /sl/ to /kl/ to blend a new word.

READING STREET ONLINE
BIG QUESTION VIDEO
www.TexasReadingStreet.com

Comprehension

Envision It!

Sequence

 READING STREET ONLINE
ENVISION IT! ANIMATIONS
www.TexasReadingStreet.com

TEKS
K.3.A.1 Identify the common sounds that letters represent. **K.3.B.2** Use letter-sound relationships to decode regular words independent of content.

Envision It! | Sounds to Know

Cc

cactus

READING STREET ONLINE ALPHABET CARDS
www.TexasReadingStreet.com

Phonics

Consonant Blends

Words I Can Blend

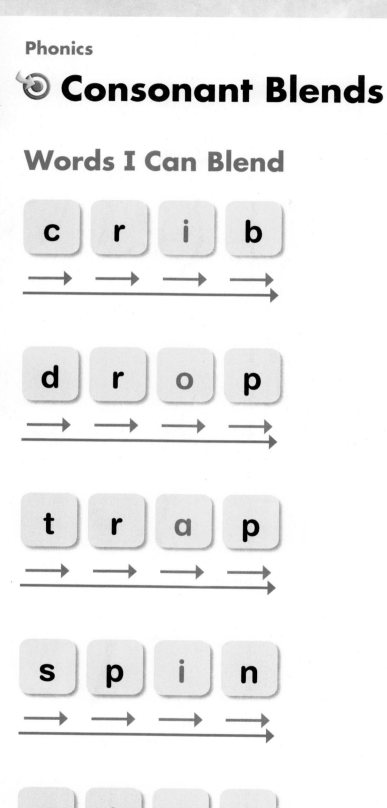

c r i b

d r o p

t r a p

s p i n

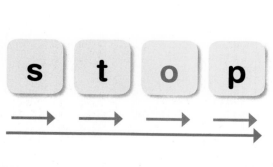

s t o p

Words I Can Read

one

two

three

four

five

Sentences I Can Read

1. One pal can spin.

2. Two can snap.

3. Can three flop?

4. I see four tots.

5. Can you do five flips?

57

TEKS

K.3.A.1 Identify the common sounds that letters represent. **K.3.B.1** Use knowledge of letter-sound relationships to decode regular words in text. **K.3.D** Identify and read at least 25 high-frequency words from a commonly used list.

Phonics

I Can Read!

Decodable Reader

- Consonant Blends

flop	spin
slam	land
drop	jump
plop	stop

- High-Frequency Words

a
one
two
three
four
five

▲ Read the story.

READING STREET ONLINE
DECODABLE eREADERS
www.TexasReadingStreet.com

One to Five

Written by Heather Leavy
Illustrated by Kris Pool

Decodable Reader 21

SPIN!

One sat on a mat.
Flop!

Two ran on a pan.
Spin! Spin!

Three hid in a lid.
Slam! Slam! Slam!

Four land on a lap.
Drop! Drop! Drop! Drop!

Five jump on top.
Plop! Plop! Plop! Plop! Plop!

Flop! Spin! Slam! Drop! Plop!

Stop! Stop! Stop!

TEKS

K.8.A.1 Retell a main event from a story read aloud. **RC-K.E.1** Retell important events in stories. **RC-K.F.2** Make connections to ideas in other texts. ★ Describe the events of a story in order.

Envision It! | Retell

Big Book

READING STREET ONLINE
STORY SORT
www.TexasReadingStreet.com

66

Think, Talk, and Write

1. How is Rooster's adventure like Little Mouse's adventure? How are they different?

Text to Text

2. What happens first in the story? What happens last?

Sequence

3. Look back and write.

67

TEKS
K.5.C Identify and sort pictures of objects into conceptual categories. K.21.A Listen attentively by facing speakers. K.22 Share information and ideas by speaking audibly and clearly using the conventions of language.

Let's

Vocabulary

- ● Where might you see heart shapes?

- ■ Look around for star shapes.

- ▲ What do you see that has an oval shape?

- ★ What do you see that has a diamond shape?

- ♥ Which shape is your favorite?

Listening and Speaking

- ● What happens first in the story?

- ■ What happens next in the story?

- ▲ Then what happens in the story?

- ★ What happens last in the story?

Words for Shapes

heart star

oval diamond

68

Listen for Sequence

Be a good listener!

69

TEKS

K.9.A.1 Identify the topic of an informational text heard. **K.11.A.1** Follow pictorial directions. **RC-K.D.3** Make inferences based on the illustrations. **RC-K.F** Make connections to own experiences and discuss textual evidence.

Make a Kazoo!

Step 1

Let's Practice It!

Directions

● Listen to the directions.

■ What do the directions tell about?

▲ What is the second step?

★ What does the boy think of his kazoo? How do you know?

♥ Tell about something you made. What did you use? What did you do?

Step 2

Step 3

Step 4

TEKS

K.2.E.1 Recognize spoken alliteration or groups of words that begin with the same spoken onset or initial sound. **K.2.F.1** Blend spoken onsets and rimes to form simple words. **K.2.H.1** Isolate the initial sound in spoken one-syllable words.

Let's Listen for

Initial Sounds

Read Together

● Point to the gate. Say the word. Say the beginning sound.

■ Find three things that begin with /g/, like *gate*.

▲ Say these words: *ball*, *grape*, *field*. Do they begin with the same sound? What about *game*, *gate*, *goal*?

★ Blend /g/ -ate. What's the word? Yes, *gate*. Change /g/ to /l/ and blend a new word.

READING STREET ONLINE
BIG QUESTION VIDEO
www.TexasReadingStreet.com

TEKS

K.6.A.2 Identify elements of a story including character. **K.8.B** Describe characters in a story and the reasons for their actions.

Comprehension

Envision It!

Literary Elements

**READING STREET ONLINE
ENVISION IT! ANIMATIONS**
www.TexasReadingStreet.com

Characters

Setting

Plot

TEKS

K.3.B.2 Use knowledge of letter-sound relationships to decode regular words independent of content.
K.3.C.1 Recognize that new words are created when letters are changed.

Gg

goose

READING STREET ONLINE
ALPHABET CARDS
www.TexasReadingStreet.com

Phonics

Initial *Gg*

Words I Can Blend

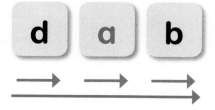

Words I Can Read

one

two

three

four

five

Sentences I Can Read

1. We can grab one bat.

2. Two hits land on the grass!

3. Brad got three hits.

4. Gil got four hits.

5. Gram can clap five claps.

TEKS

K.3.A.1 Identify the common sounds that letters represent. **K.3.B.1** Use knowledge of letter-sound relationships to decode regular words in text. **K.3.D** Identify and read at least 25 high-frequency words from a commonly used list.

Phonics

I Can Read!

Decodable Reader

- Consonant *Gg*
  Gil
  got
  flag

- ■ High-Frequency Words
  one
  two
  three
  four
  five
  a
  is

- ▲ Read the story.

READING STREET ONLINE
DECODABLE eREADERS
www.TexasReadingStreet.com

Gil Got One

Written by William Dillberts
Illustrated by Hillary Gem

Decodable Reader 22

Gil got one.
Pop!
Sad Gil.

Gil got two.
Pop! Pop!
Sad Gil.

Gil got three.
Pop! Pop! Pop!
Sad Gil.

Gil got four.
Pop! Pop! Pop! Pop!
Sad Gil.

Gil got five.
Pop! Pop! Pop! Pop! Pop!
Sad Gil.

Mom had a plan.
Mom got Gil a flag.

Gil is not sad.

TEKS

K.6.A.2 Identify elements of a story including character. **K.8.A.1** Retell a main event from a story read aloud. **K.8.B.1** Describe characters in a story.

Envision It! Retell

Goldilocks and the Three Bears
Retold and illustrated by Valeri Gorbachev

Trade Book

READING STREET ONLINE
STORY SORT
www.TexasReadingStreet.com

Think, Talk, and Write

1. What do you think Goldilocks learned? *Text to World*

2. Which is a character from *Goldilocks and the Three Bears?*

 Character

3. Look back and write.

TEKS

K.5.B Recognize that compound words are made up of shorter words. **K.22** Share information and ideas by speaking audibly and clearly using the conventions of language.

Let's Learn It!

Vocabulary

- Talk about the pictures.
- Blend the words *bed* and *room*.
- ▲ Segment the word *tiptoe*.

Listening and Speaking

- Would you rather be an author or an illustrator? Tell why.

Vocabulary

Compound Words

bed + room =

bedroom

tip + toe = tiptoe

Discuss Authors and Illustrators

title

author

illustrator

Be a good speaker!

TEKS

K.6.A Identify elements of a story including characters and setting. **K.6.B** Discuss the big idea of a well-known folk tale and connect it to personal experience. **K.6.D** Recognize recurring phrases and characters in traditional folk tales from various cultures.

Let's Practice It!

Folk Tale

● Listen to the folk tale.

■ How does the story begin?

▲ When and where does the story take place?

★ How are these characters like the ones in "The Three Little Pigs"?

♥ What lesson does the folk tale teach? Share ideas about how the lesson can help you.

How the Fly Saved the River

TEKS

K.2.E.1 Recognize spoken alliteration or groups of words that begin with the same spoken onset or initial sound. **K.2.H.1** Isolate the initial sound in spoken one-syllable words.

Phonemic Awareness

Let's Listen for

Initial Sounds

Read Together

- Say *Ed.* What sound do you hear at the beginning of *Ed?*

- Find three things that begin with /e/, like *Ed.*

- Name other words that begin with /e/.

- Say these words: *Ed, elm, engine.* Do they begin the same? What about *end, clown, egg?*

READING STREET ONLINE
BIG QUESTION VIDEO
www.TexasReadingStreet.com

DINER

Comprehension

Envision It!

Classify and Categorize

READING STREET ONLINE
ENVISION IT! ANIMATIONS
www.TexasReadingStreet.com

TEKS

K.3.B Use knowledge of letter-sound relationships to decode regular words in text and independent of content.
K.3.D.1 Identify and read at least 25 high-frequency words from a commonly used list.

Envision It! | Sounds to Know

Ee

escalator

READING STREET ONLINE
ALPHABET CARDS
www.TexasReadingStreet.com

Phonics

Short e

Words I Can Blend

h e n

r e d

B e n

f e d

s e t

Words I Can Read

here

go

from

Sentences I Can Read

1. Ben is here.

2. We go to see Meg.

3. The hen is from Meg.

TEKS

K.3.A.1 Identify the common sounds that letters represent. **K.3.B.1** Use knowledge of letter-sound relationships to decode regular words in text. **K.3.D** Identify and read at least 25 high-frequency words from a commonly used list.

Phonics

Decodable Reader

● Short *Ee*

get	Red
Hen	Ben
pen	Ken
Len	

■ High-Frequency Words

go
the
from
here

▲ Read the story.

**READING STREET ONLINE
DECODABLE eREADERS**
www.TexasReadingStreet.com

Decodable Reader 23

Red Hen

Written by Nathan Aguilera
Illustrated by Samantha Johnson

Get Red Hen, Ben.
Red Hen can go in the pen.

Red Hen ran from Ben.
Red Hen hid here.

Red Hen did not get in the pen.

Get Red Hen, Ken.
Red Hen can go in the pen.

Red Hen ran from Ken.
Red Hen hid here.

Red Hen did not get in the pen.

Len got Red Hen!

TEKS

K.10.B.1 Retell important facts in a text, heard or read. **RC-K.F.1** Make connections to own experiences. **RC-K.F.4** Discuss textual evidence.

Envision It! | Retell

Big Book

1

2

3

4

5

6

READING STREET ONLINE
STORY SORT
www.TexasReadingStreet.com

Think, Talk, and Write

1. What would you like to do on an Antarctic adventure? **Text to Self**

2. Which does not belong in Antarctica?

Classify and Categorize

3. Look back and write.

TEKS

K.5.A Identify and use words that name directions. **K.21.A.1** Listen attentively by facing speakers.

Let's Learn It!

Vocabulary

- ● Talk about the pictures.
- ■ Point to north on the map.
- ▲ Now point to south, east, and west.

Listening and Speaking

- ● Name the characters in the stories.

Vocabulary

Direction Words

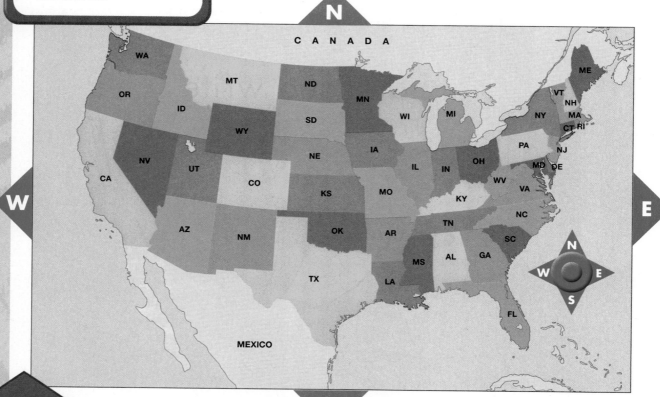

Listen for Story Elements
Character

Be a good listener!

TEKS
K.2.C.1 Orally generate rhymes in response to spoken words. **K.7A** Respond to rhythm and rhyme in poetry through identifying a regular beat and similarities in word sounds. **RC-K.A** Discuss purposes for reading and listening to various texts.

One, Two, Buckle My Shoe

Let's Practice It!

Nursery Rhyme

- Listen to the rhyme.

- Say the rhyme. Clap your hands to show each beat.

- Which words rhyme? Name another word that rhymes with each pair.

- Why do children like to read and listen to nursery rhymes?

TEKS

K.2.F.1 Blend spoken onsets and rimes to form simple words. K.2.H.1 Isolate the initial sound in spoken one-syllable words.

Phonemic Awareness

Let's Listen for

Read Together

Initial Sounds

● Say the sound you hear at the beginning of *elephant, hat, leaf, girl, flag, star, crowd.*

■ Point to the elephant. Find something that begins like *elephant.*

▲ Now find pictures that begin with /h/, /l/, /g/, /fl/, /st/, and /kr/.

★ Name other words that begin with /e/, /h/, /l/, /g/, /fl/, /st/, and /kr/.

♥ Blend /h/ -*at.* What's the word? Yes, *hat.* Now change /h/ to /fl/ to make a new word.

READING STREET ONLINE
BIG QUESTION VIDEO
www.TexasReadingStreet.com

112

Comprehension

Envision It!

Literary Elements

READING STREET ONLINE
ENVISION IT! ANIMATIONS
www.TexasReadingStreet.com

Characters

Setting

Plot

115

TEKS

K.3.B Use letter-sound relationships to decode regular words in text and independent of content.
K.3.C.1 Recognize that new words are created when letters are changed.

Ee

escalator

READING STREET ONLINE
ALPHABET CARDS
www.TexasReadingStreet.com

Phonics

Short e

Words I Can Blend

b e d

r e d

f e d

f e l l

t e l l

116

Words I Can Read

here

go

from

Sentences I Can Read

1. My dad is here.
2. I go to help him.
3. The pen is from Mom.

TEKS

K.3.A.1 Identify the common sounds that letters represent. **K.3.B.1** Use knowledge of letter-sound relationships to decode regular words in text. **K.3.D** Identify and read at least 25 high-frequency words from a commonly used list.

Phonics

Decodable Reader

● Short *Ee*

Peg	met
Ned	pet
Hen	pen
bed	get
fed	let

■ High-Frequency Words

a
from
here
is
have
go

▲ Read the story.

**READING STREET ONLINE
DECODABLE eREADERS**
www.TexasReadingStreet.com

A Pet Hen

Written by Fran Quinn
Illustrated by Jason Edwards

Decodable Reader 24

Peg met Ned.
Peg got a pet from Ned.
Here is Hen.

Did Hen have a pen?
Hen did not.

Peg got Hen a pen.
Go in, Hen.

Did Hen have a bed?
Hen did not.

Peg got Hen a bed.
Get in, Hen.

Peg fed Hen.

Peg got in bed.
Let Peg nap, Hen.

TEKS

K.6.A.1 Identify elements of a story including setting. **K.8.A.1** Retell a main event from a story read aloud. **RC-K.E.1** Retell important events in stories. **RC-K.F.3** Make connections to the larger community.

Envision It! | Retell

Trade Book

READING STREET ONLINE
STORY SORT
www.TexasReadingStreet.com

126

Think, Talk, and Write

1. Why is Rosalba and Abuela's adventure special? How can others have such an adventure? **Text to World**

2. Where does the story *Abuela* take place?

Setting

3. Look back and write.

127

TEKS

K.21.A Listen attentively by facing speakers and asking questions to clarify information. **K.23.A.2** Follow agreed-upon rules for discussion, including speaking one at a time.

Vocabulary

- ● Talk about the picture.
- ■ What day of the week is it today?
- ▲ In what month is your birthday?

Listening and Speaking

- ● Say some words from a poem, song, or nursery rhyme.

Vocabulary

Time Words

Month

March

Sunday	Monday	Tuesday	Wednesday	Thursday	Friday	Saturday
Day		1	2	3	4	5
6	7	8	9	10	11	12
13	14	15	16	17	18	19
Week 20	21	22	23	24	25	26
27	28	29	30	31		

128

Listen to Poems

Be a good listener!

TEKS

K.4.B.1 Ask questions about texts read aloud. **K.10.A** Identify the topic and details in expository text heard or read, referring to the words. **K.10.C.1** Discuss the way authors group information in text. **RC-K.B** Ask and respond to questions about text.

Let's Practice It!

Expository Text

● Listen to the selection. What is it about?

■ Who gave the statue to the people of the United States?

▲ What information did the author tell about first? next? and last?

★ What details, or special facts, does the author tell us about what the statue looks like?

♥ What questions does the selection make you want to ask?

The Statue of Liberty

1

Words for Things That Go

airplane

bike

truck

car

bus

van

boat

train

Words for Colors

white

purple

brown

green

pink

black

blue

red

yellow

orange

Words for Shapes

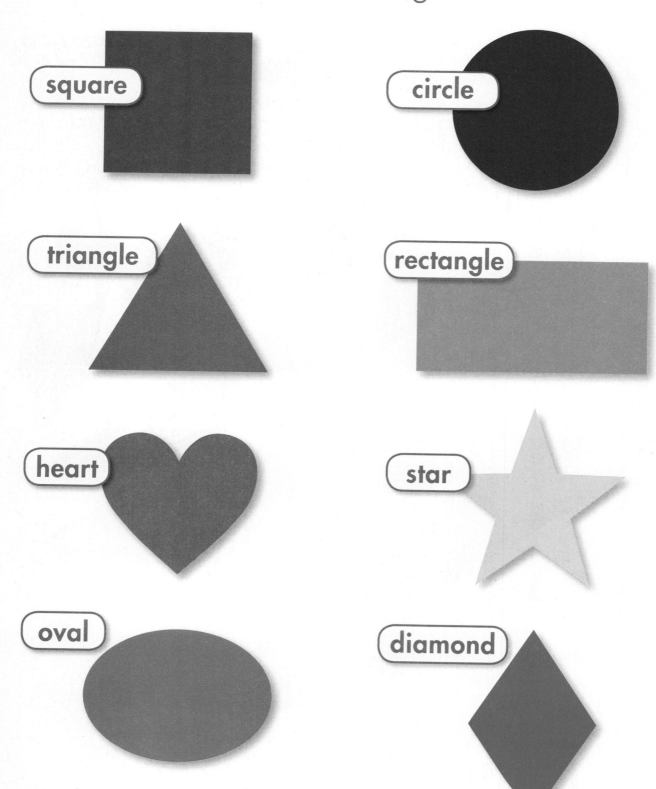

square

circle

triangle

rectangle

heart

star

oval

diamond

Words for Places

school

home

park

train station

police station

fire station

post office

library

Words for Animals

lion

mouse

puppy

dog

cat

duck

turtle

kitten

chick

hen

rooster

bird

136

butterfly

fish

whale

caterpillar

bear

panda

beaver

calf

cow

Words for Actions

skip

walk

run

fly

swim

ride

jump

hop

Position Words

up

down

in

out

on

around

over

under

My Classroom

bookcase

easel

books

desk

markers

crayons

pencils

teacher

toys

paper

chair

blocks

table

rug

Words for Feelings

happy

frightened

worried

excited

angry

proud

sad

surprised

My Family

mom
mother

dad
father

sister

grandmother

grandfather

brother

Acknowledgments

Illustrations

Cover: Rob Hefferan

12 Manja Stojic

19–25 Cale Atkinson

28, 49, 69, 88, 129 George Ulrich

30 Jan Bryan Hunt

32 Aaron Zenz

39–45 Natalia Vasquez

50–51 Steve Mack

52 Marilyn Janovitz

59–65 Dani Jones

72 Steve Simpson

90–91 Jason Wolff

92 Ron Lieser

99–105 Robbie Short

110–111 Vanessa Newton

112 Karol Kaminski

119–125 Wednesday Kirwan.

The *Texas Essential Knowledge and Skills for English Language Arts and Reading* reproduced by permission, Texas Education Agency, 1701 N. Congress Avenue, Austin, TX 78701

Photographs

Every effort has been made to secure permission and provide appropriate credit for photographic material. The publisher deeply regrets any omission and pledges to correct errors called to its attention in subsequent editions.

Unless otherwise acknowledged, all photographs are the property of Pearson Education, Inc.

Photo locators denoted as follows: Top (T), Center (C), Bottom (B), Left (L), Right (R), Background (Bkgd)

10 (B) ©Mario Lopes/Alamy

48 ©Andy Sands/Nature Picture Library, ©Envision/Corbis, ©Fusion Pix/Corbis, Dave King/©DK Images

130 (B) ©Thinkstock/Corbis

131 (C) ©Jochen Tack/Peter Arnold, Inc., (T, B) ©Peter Bennett/Ambient Images, Inc., (TL) PhotoLibrary Group, Ltd.